UKULELE
GRACE VANDERWAAL
JUST THE BEGINNING

ISBN 978-1-5400-2038-3

7777 W. BLUEMOUND RD. P.O. BOX 13819 MILWAUKEE, WI 53213

In Australia Contact:
Hal Leonard Australia Pty. Ltd.
4 Lentara Court
Cheltenham, Victoria, 3192 Australia
Email: ausadmin@halleonard.com.au

Visit Hal Leonard Online at
www.halleonard.com

CONTENTS

Moonlight

Words and Music by Grace VanderWaal and Ido Zmishlany

First note

Verse
Moderately bright

1. She al-ways has a smile ___ from morn-ing to the night. ___ The
2. Now she lost her way ___ and she for-gets to smile. ___

per - fect pos - ter child ___ that was once in my life. ___ }
Nev - er gets a break ___ from this life in de - nial. ___ }

A

doll made out of glass, ___ all her friends think that she's great. ___ But

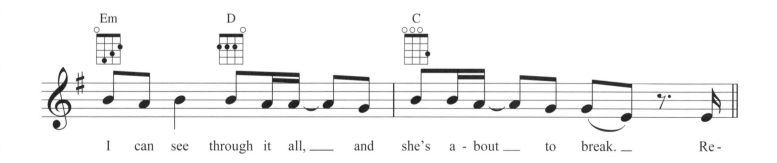

I can see through it all, ___ and she's a - bout ___ to break. ___ Re -

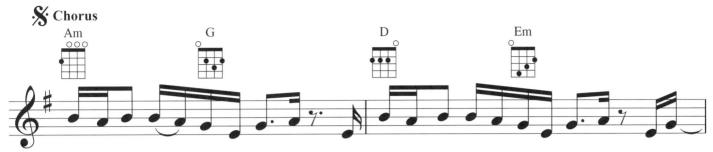

mem-ber last year __ when you told me to al-ways stay here and nev-er leave me? The light __

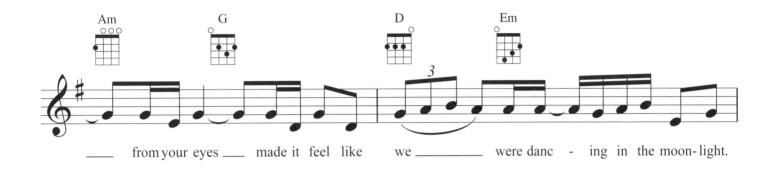

__ from your eyes __ made it feel like we _____ were danc - ing in the moon-light.

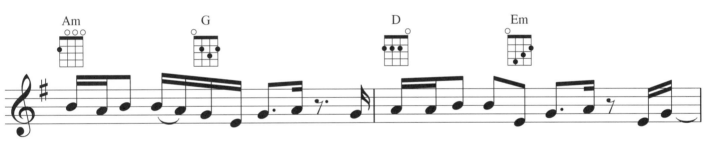

'Mem-ber last year __ when you told me that these would be life-long sto - ries? The light __

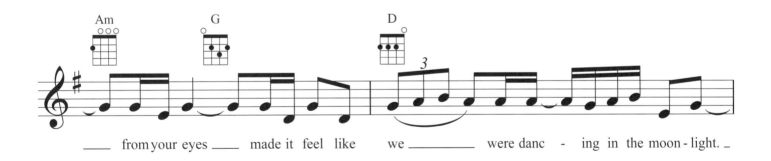

__ from your eyes __ made it feel like we _____ were danc - ing in the moon-light. __

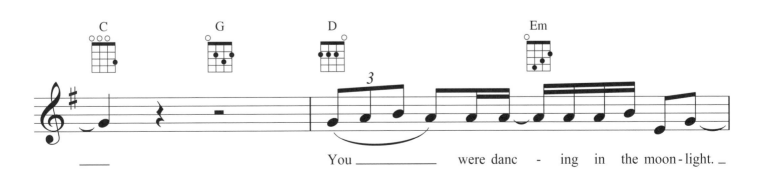

__ You _____ were danc - ing in the moon-light. __

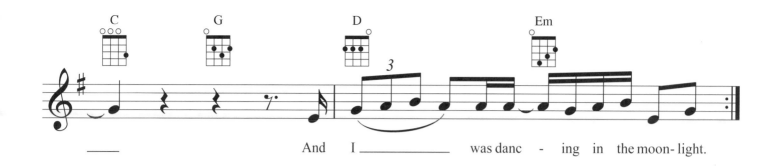

And I _____ was danc - ing in the moon - light.

Bridge

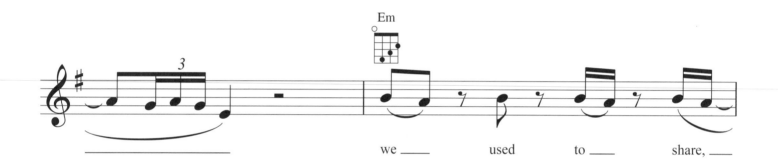

I, ___ I, I _____ miss those mem - o - ries ___

_____ we ___ used to ___ share, ___

___ just you and me. _____ I re-

* Let chord ring.

Outro-Chorus

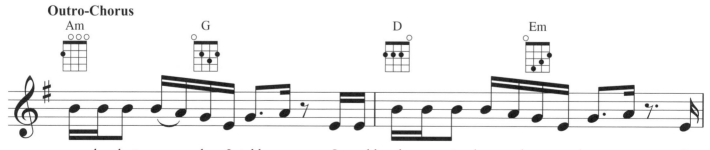

mem-ber last year _ when I told you I would al - ways stay here and nev - er leave you. I

told you the light in your eyes made it look like we _____ were danc - ing in the moon-light. ___
Re-

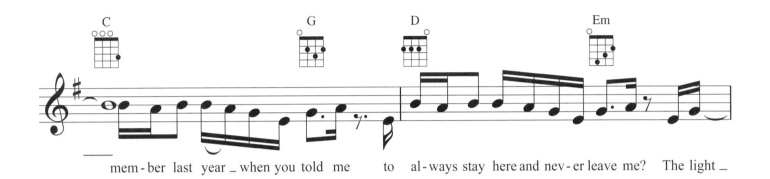

mem - ber last year _ when you told me to al - ways stay here and nev - er leave me? The light _

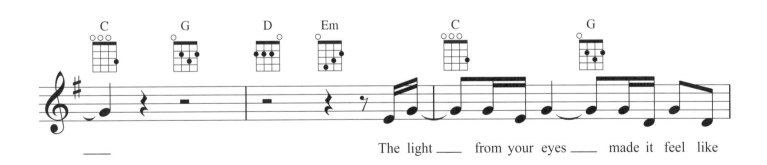

___ from your eyes ___ made it feel like we _____ were danc - ing in the moon - light _

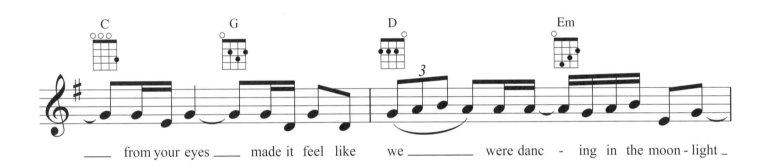

The light ___ from your eyes ___ made it feel like

danc - ing in the moon - light. _____

Sick of Being Told

Words and Music by Grace VanderWaal, Jeremy Dussolliet and Tim Sommers

Escape My Mind

Words and Music by Grace VanderWaal, Gregg Wattenberg and Michael Adubato

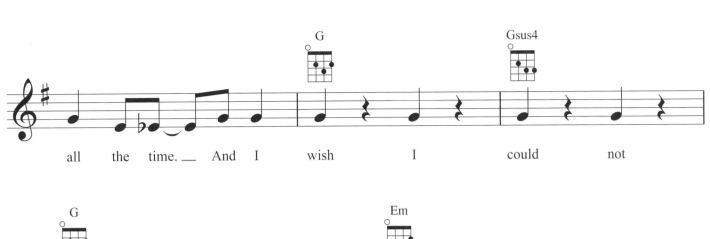

all   the   time.   And   I   wish   I   could   not

think,   for   once   in   my   life,   but

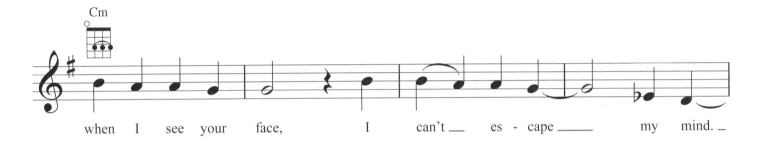

when   I   see   your   face,   I   can't   es - cape   my   mind.

Verse

To Coda

2. I   know   we   were   nev - er   a

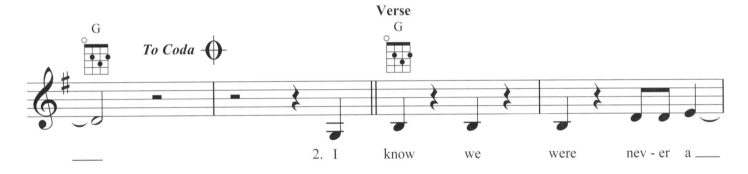

thing,   but   I   al - ways   think   a - bout

what   could   have   hap - pened   if   we   kept   go - ing.   And   I

nev - er had this hap - pen to me. ___

On - ly in the mov - ies, _____ but,

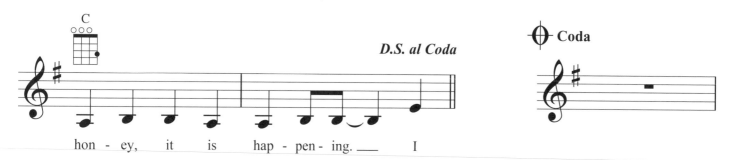

D.S. al Coda

⊕ Coda

hon - ey, it is hap - pen - ing. ___ I

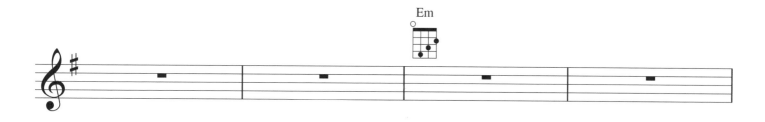

Bridge

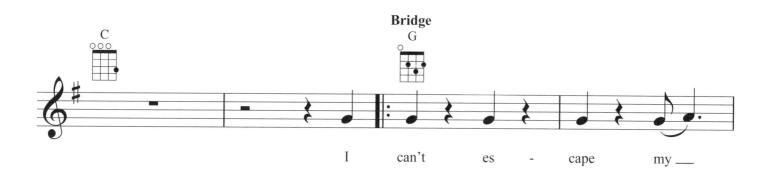

I can't es - cape my ___

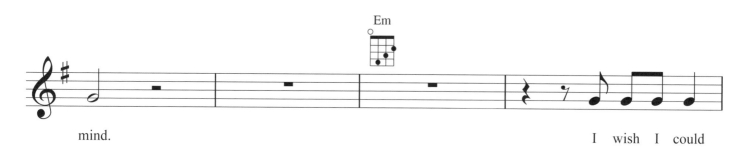

mind.

I wish I could

Burned

Words and Music by Grace VanderWaal and Sean Douglas

* *Recorded a whole step lower.*

don't play with fi - re, but you're al - read - y burned, _ you're al - read - y burned. _

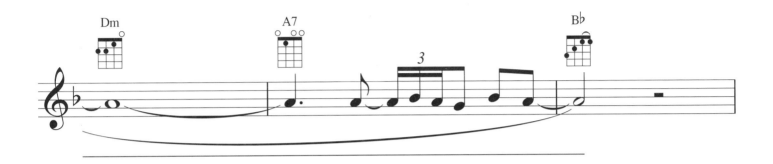

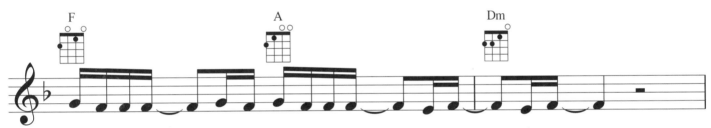

Wan-na get burned, _ wan-na, wan-na get burned, _ (get burned, _ get burned.) _

Wan-na get burned, _ wan-na, wan-na get burned, _ (get burned, _ get burned.)

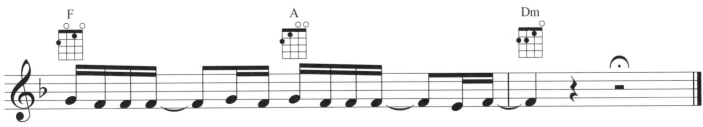

Wan-na get burned, _ wan - na, wan-na get burned, _ get burned. _

Just a Crush

Words and Music by Grace VanderWaal

like   what you're _ search-ing   for, _____   oh. _____   You're

Chorus

just, _____   just, _____

To Coda ⊕

just, _____   you   are,   you __ are   just a   crush. _

Verse

N.C.

___   2. I   hope   you   un - der - stand ____

what   I'm __ tell - ing   you.   I   don't   wan - na

be   con - fus - ing.   Con - sid - er   me   one   of   the

So Much More Than This

Words and Music by Grace VanderWaal, Derek Fuhrmann and Gregg Wattenberg

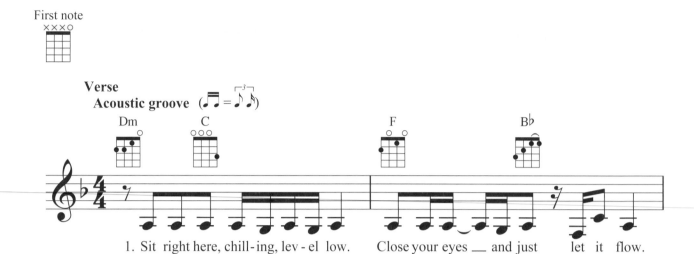

1. Sit right here, chill-ing, lev-el low. Close your eyes __ and just let it flow.

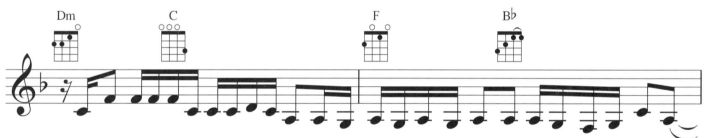

Right next to me I hear your heart beat, beat when the dial turns up and the mu-sic starts play-ing.

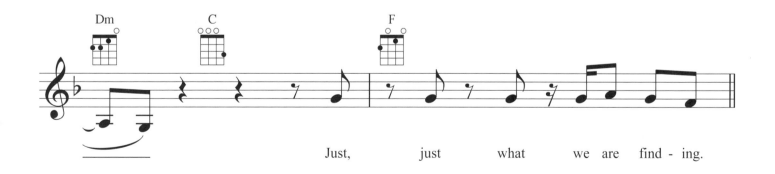

We don't re-al-ize in this so-ci-e-ty, does-n't mat-ter how your hair looks or what they are think-ing. __

Just, just what we are find-ing.

Tap your foot and lis - ten in. Ig - nore the world, __ let the mu - sic cave __ in.

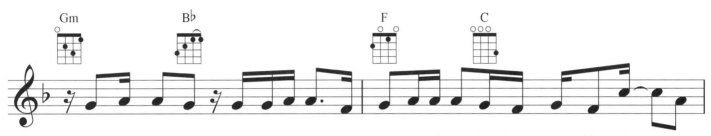

Close your phone and breathe in the air. You'll soon re - al - ize that there's some - thing that __ is

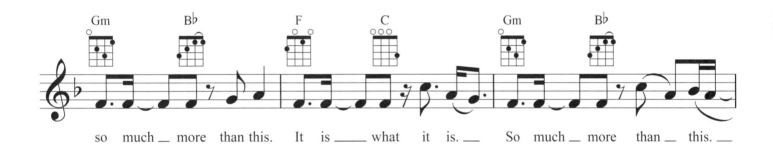

so much __ more than this. It is ___ what it is. __ So much __ more than __ this. __

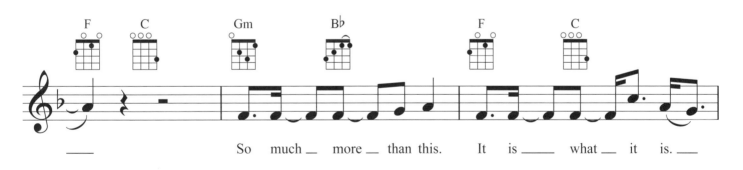

___ So much __ more __ than this. It is ___ what __ it is. __

To Coda 1
To Coda 2

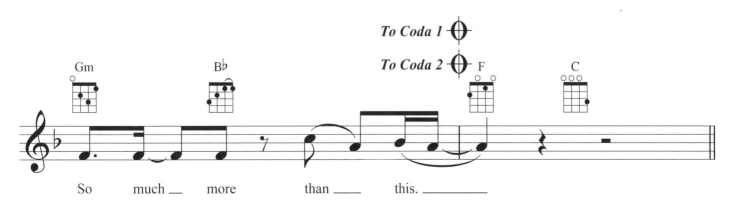

So much __ more than ___ this. _____

Verse

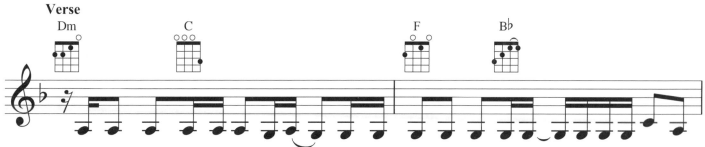

2. The whole crowd seems to like me now __ 'cause they think I'm cool, but back __ when I was in school,

they found it ver-y eas - y to hate me. Fun-ny how al - ways these times are chang - ing.

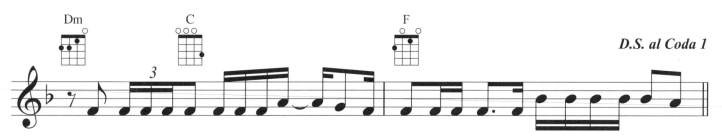

D.S. al Coda 1

Back then it was so eas-y to shat - ter, but now in the end, it does-n't real - ly mat - ter.

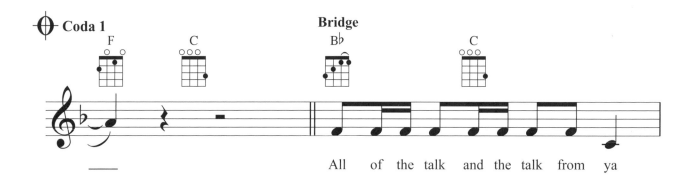

⊕ Coda 1

Bridge

____ All of the talk and the talk from ya

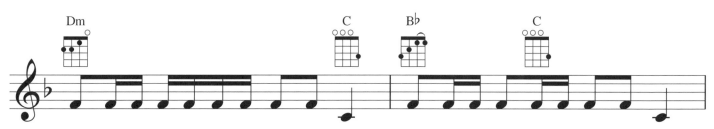

won't e - ven mat - ter when the lights come up. All of the talk and the talk from ya.

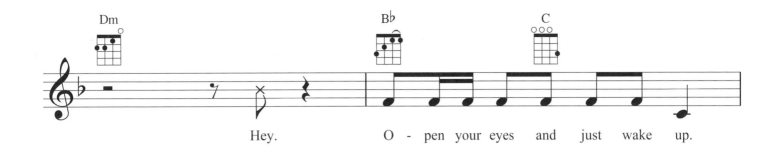

Hey. O - pen your eyes and just wake up.

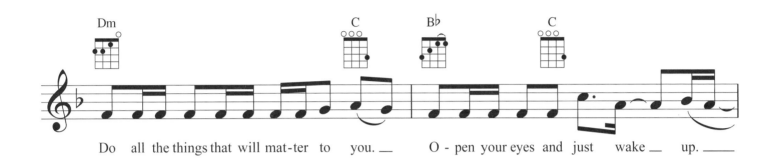

Do all the things that will mat-ter to you. O - pen your eyes and just wake up.

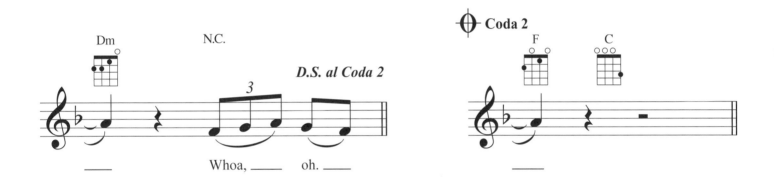

D.S. al Coda 2

Coda 2

Whoa, oh.

Outro-Chorus

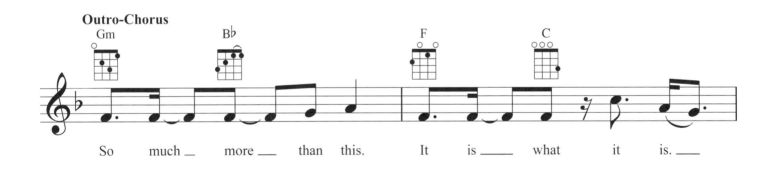

So much more than this. It is what it is.

So much more than this. Oh, oh, oh, oh, oh, oh.

Talk Good

Words and Music by Grace VanderWaal and Ido Zmishlany

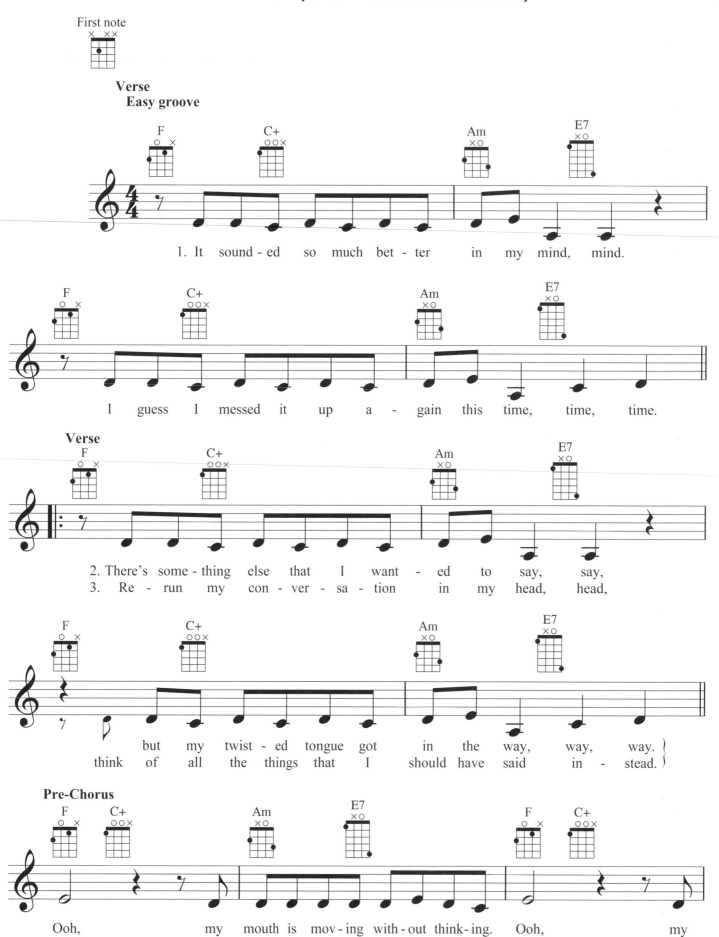

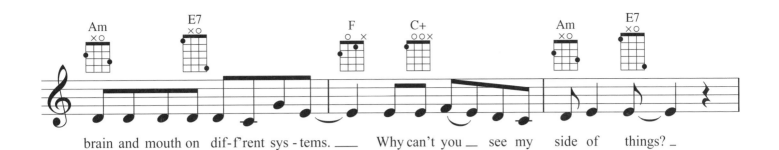

brain and mouth on dif-f'rent sys-tems. ___ Why can't you ___ see my side of things? _

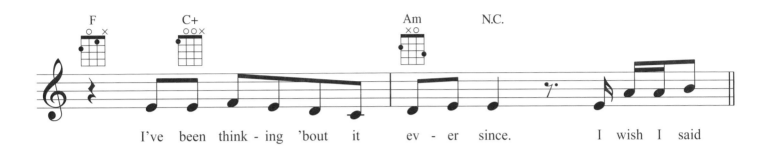

I've been think-ing 'bout it ev-er since. I wish I said

Chorus

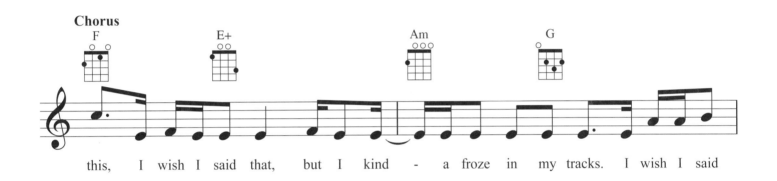

this, I wish I said that, but I kind - a froze in my tracks. I wish I said

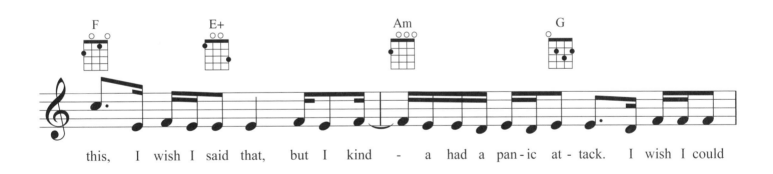

this, I wish I said that, but I kind - a had a pan-ic at - tack. I wish I could

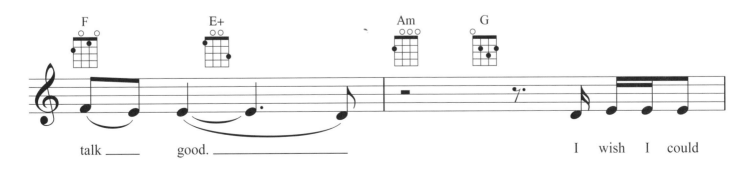

talk ___ good. ___ I wish I could

talk,   I wish I could talk,   I wish I could   talk ____ good.

talk ____ good. ____ I wish I could talk ____ good. _____

I wish I could   talk,   I wish I could talk,   I wish I could

Bridge

talk __ good.   My words, __ my mind ____ are worth all your time.

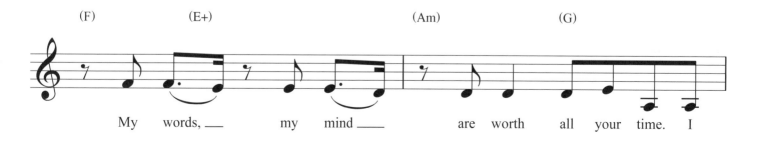

My words, ___ my mind ____ are worth all your time. I

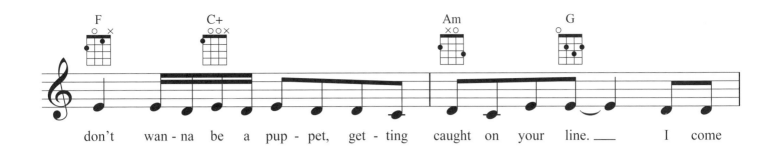

don't wan - na be a pup - pet, get - ting caught on your line. ___ I come

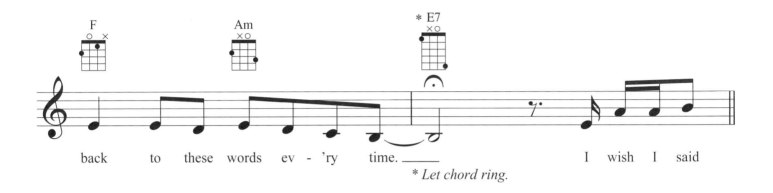

back to these words ev - 'ry time. _____ I wish I said

Let chord ring.

Outro-Chorus

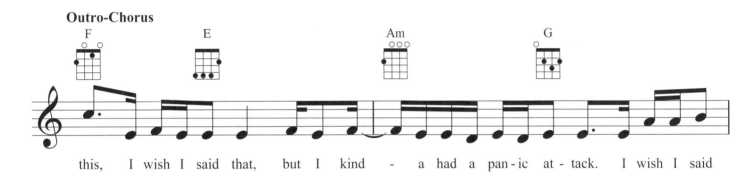

this, I wish I said that, but I kind - a had a pan - ic at - tack. I wish I said

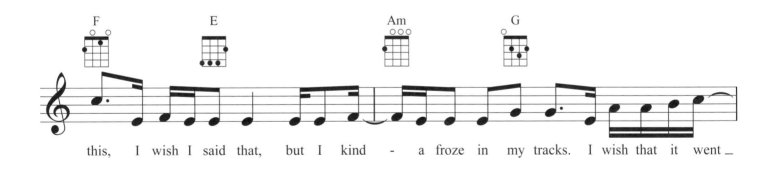

this, I wish I said that, but I kind - a froze in my tracks. I wish that it went ___

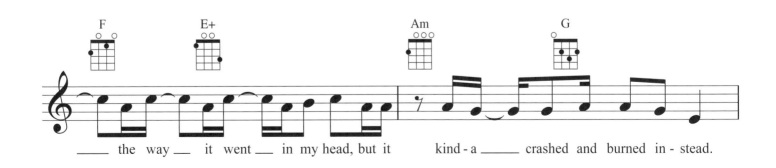

____ the way ___ it went ___ in my head, but it kind - a _____ crashed and burned in - stead.

Why does it al-ways end up like this? And I so ___ bad-ly wish I could

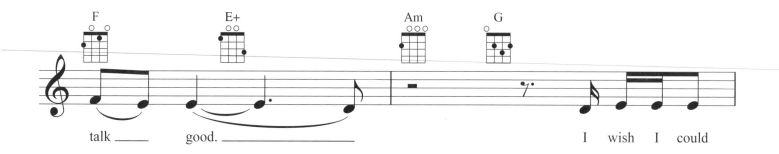

talk ___ good. ___ I wish I could

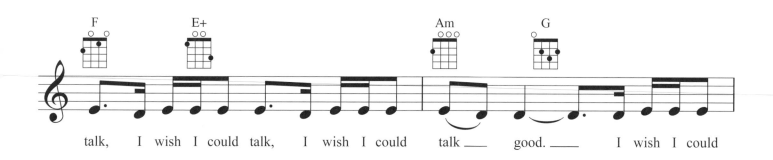

talk, I wish I could talk, I wish I could talk ___ good. ___ I wish I could

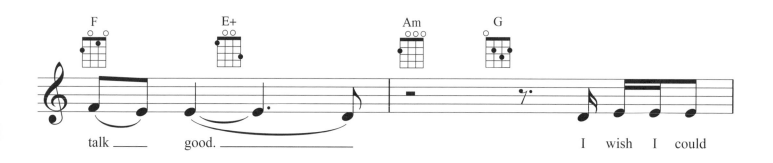

talk ___ good. ___ I wish I could

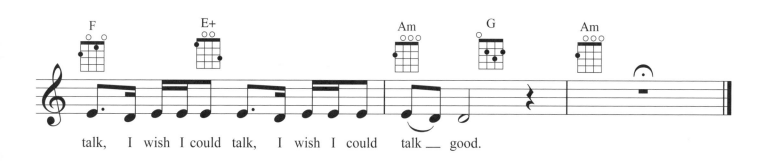

talk, I wish I could talk, I wish I could talk ___ good.

Florets

Words and Music by Grace VanderWaal and Ido Zmishlany

* Recorded a half step lower.

then you should _ know _____ that we could just be

𝄋 **Chorus**

blow - ing flo - rets. I wan - na

dance in the air, blow - ing flo -

rets, and just not _ care a - bout an - y - one _____ or

an - y - thing ___ but you ___ and me, so

don't let go ___ of me. _____

Insane Sometimes

Words and Music by Grace VanderWaal and Dan Henig

the __ walls. _____ *(Instrumental)* So,

Coda all a lit-tle in-sane some-times? _ *(Instrumental)* **Bridge**

Don't you know, _

___ ooh, _____ ooh, _____ we're

all a lit-tle in-sane some-times? _ Spin the

Chorus

rec-ord, __ dar-ling, in-side of my mind, __ and let's just

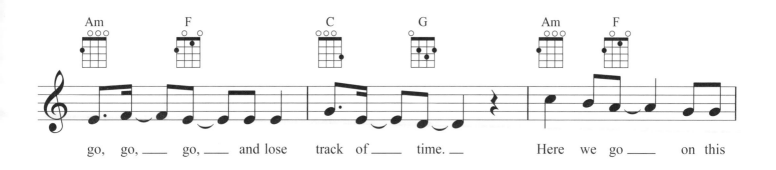

go, go, ___ go, ___ and lose track of ___ time. ___ Here we go ___ on this

cra - zy ride. ___ Here we go ___ in this cra - zy life, ___ ooh, oh. ___

___ 'Cause, 'cause, don't you know _____ we're

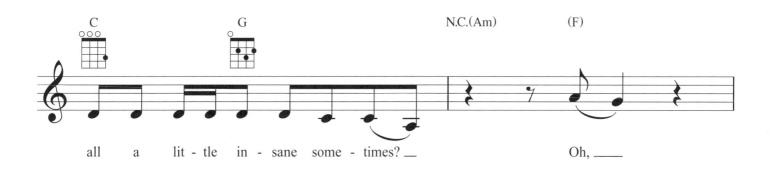

all a lit - tle in - sane some - times? ___ Oh, ___

oh. _____ We're all a lit - tle in - sane some - times. _

A Better Life

Words and Music by Grace VanderWaal

a

bet - ter ___ life, ___ mm. ___

To Coda ⊕

Verse

2. You found a light - er

on the street,

and sud - den - ly ev - 'ry - thing just seemed so

hap - py. ___ mm. ___

bet - ter life. ___ Let the wind blow ___ through your hair, ___

___ let ___ the mu - sic ___ take you there, ___ and

make _____ a

bet - ter ___ life, ___ a bet - ter ___ life. ___

___ May - be this ___ time ___

things will turn ___ out right. ___

City Song

Words and Music by Grace VanderWaal, Gregg Wattenberg and Michael Adubato

Recorded a half step lower.

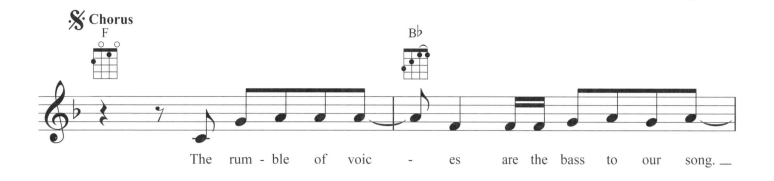

The rum - ble of voic - es are the bass to our song. ___

___ The horns are just on ___ the beat, honk - in' a - long. ___

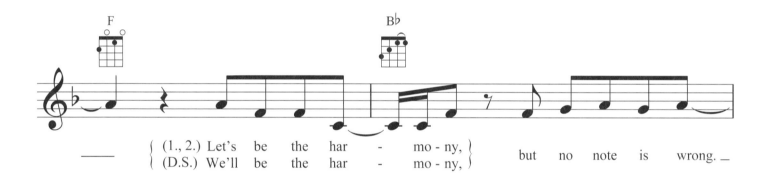

___ { (1., 2.) Let's be the har - mo - ny, }
      { (D.S.) We'll be the har - mo - ny, } but no note is wrong. ___

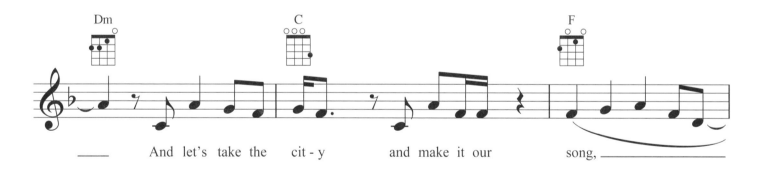

___ And let's take the cit - y and make it our song, ___

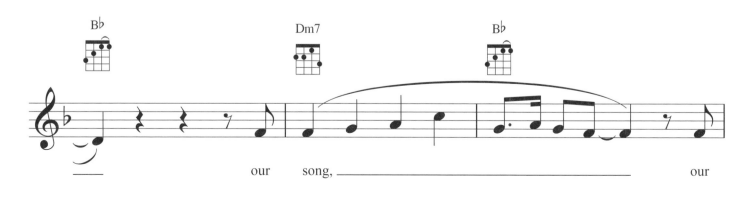

___ our song, _____ our

song. _____ Let's take ___ the cit-y and make it our

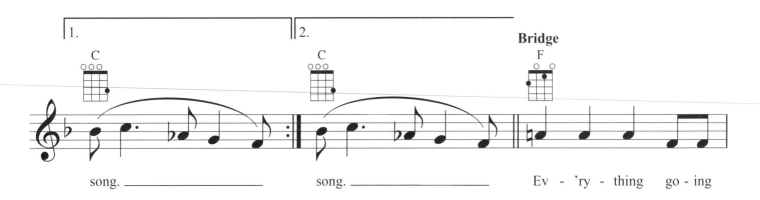

1.

song. _____

2.

song. _____

Bridge

Ev-'ry-thing go-ing

on a-round ___ you, ___ just

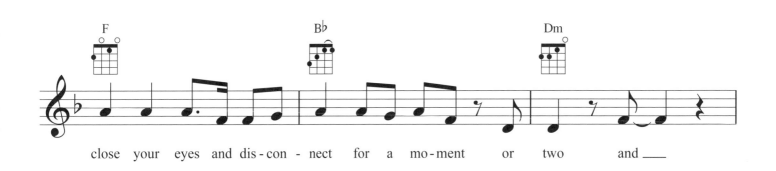

close your eyes and dis-con-nect for a mo-ment or two and ___

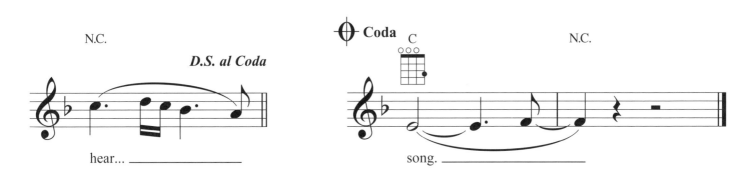

N.C.

D.S. al Coda

hear... _____

Coda

C

N.C.

song. _____

Darkness Keeps Chasing Me

Words and Music by Grace VanderWaal and Micah Premnath

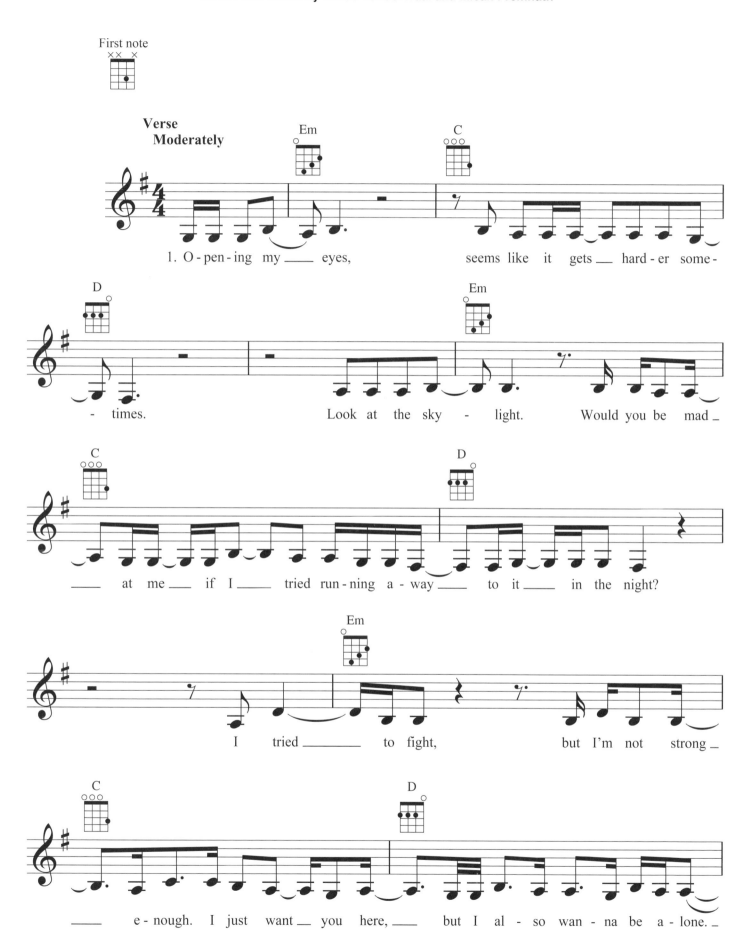

Don't tell me you __ fell __ in; the dark - ness is

al - read - y seep - ing through. __ Oh, can't you __ see? _____

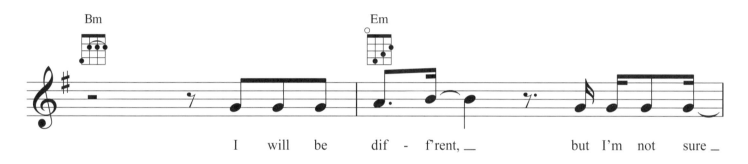

I will be dif - f'rent, __ but I'm not sure __

__ if I __ can do it all __ a - lone. __

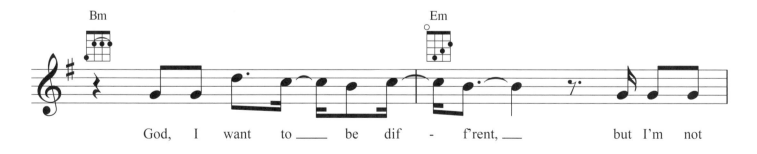

God, I want to __ be dif - f'rent, __ but I'm not

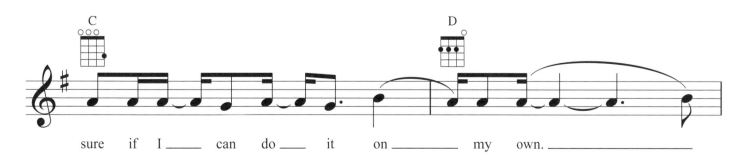

sure if I __ can do __ it on __ my own. _____

wan - na give up ____ that eas - i - ly, ____

but the dark - ness ____ keeps chas - ing

me, ____

me, ____

me, ____

me. ____

I Don't Know My Name

Words and Music by Grace VanderWaal

get a - long quite nice - ly. You

ask me why I cut my hair and

changed my - self com - plete - ly.

𝄋 Chorus
Moderately fast

I don't know my name.

I don't play by the

rules ____ of the game. ____ So you say

I'm just _____ try - ing,

just try - ing. _____ 2. I

Verse
Very fast

rit.

went from bland and pop - u - lar to

Moderately fast

join - ing the march - ing _____ band. I

made the clos - est friends I'll ev - er

have in my _____ life - time. _____